Introduction

We live in a world where no one respects their time. We have so little of it, and yet we waste it, playing games on our phones, watching reruns of shows that we've already seen, and countless hours of gossip about celebrities or things that a neighbor has that we think would make us happier.

All through this, we are stuck with the feeling that something is wrong. Sure, we might have goals, but the trend is to collect them, not to achieve them, and in the end, there is the genuine fear that we'll pass without so much as rippling the pond.

Stoicism is the cure for this. It is a philosophy that teaches many things, including:

- Stifling those emotional, knee-jerk responses that lead to bad decision making

- Learning to hoard your time so that you can allocate it properly
- The ability to appreciate the things that you have
- The wisdom in embracing your past and having no fear of death
- How to define yourself with your actions, rather than your words or your possessions

These are just a few examples, but there are many, many more. For instance, you simply cannot insult a Stoic. Through exercises and the application of ancient wisdom, the Stoic knows the proper way to perceive these things. This is not a gimmick or some sort of trick. For instance, if I criticize your work, as a Stoic, your first thought would not be "my work was inferior" but rather, "is the criticism correct?" because if it IS, then the person giving you the criticism has done you a favor.

It's all about perception, and in this book, we will teach you how to shape yours so that it serves you instead of harming you.

You are probably wondering at this point, "why should I believe you?", and as an aspiring Stoic, that is a good approach. Always analyze. Well, the reason that Stoicism is as powerful an approach in the modern-day as it was in ancient Greece is simply this.

It works.

As you read this, people around the world are reading the wisdom of philosophers such as Seneca, Marcus Aurelius, Epictetus, Socrates, and more. If you haven't had the pleasure of the original texts, know that you will get a taste of this inside so that you can see what all of this is about. The simple truth is that these words have been translated numerous times and published around the world because they were viable in the past.

And they are still viable NOW. As the quaint old saying goes, "If it ain't broke, don't fix it."

While these words have been around since before Biblical times, your time to start discovering them and using them is brief.

So, get started on reading this <u>right now</u>!

Remember, you cannot own possessions, even your body is only "loaned" to you, but you can own your own reason and your happiness.

Read further and we'll show you how!

Chapter 1 Being A Stoic Is Not Easy

So, you want to be a Stoic? The rewards are substantial when you adopt this powerful philosophy that predates Christ. We need to establish now that this is NOT an easy path. If you are willing to make an effort and "put in the time" that it takes to reshape your personal views to include Stoicism, then the rewards are countless. Epictetus said it best in his famous Discourses:

"With rewards this substantial, be aware that a casual effort is not sufficient. Other ambitions will have to be sacrificed, altogether or at least for now. If you want these rewards at the same time that you are striving for power and riches, chances are you will not get to be rich and powerful while you aim for the other goal; and the rewards of freedom and happiness will elude you altogether." [1]

What's it going to be? Can you put in the time that it takes to reshape your behavior? In becoming a Stoic, you will need to learn, above all things, to analyze the things which you come into contact with. A Stoic can recognize the difference between an influence of nature, which cannot be changed, and the things that may be influenced by your will.

Simply put, the key to your own happiness is within you and to get it you must learn to:

- Recognize external influences that are beyond your control
- Exercise your will and judgment on those things which you CAN control

This seemingly simple core of Stoicism is easy to understand but to practice? That is quite another thing. The Stoics believed that this discipline must be manifest in your actions rather than your words. We recommend that you try to master one principle at a time, rather than to try and absorb them all at once. This is a difficult philosophy to master, so be sure that you are always focusing on learning a Stoic principle.

Some examples of behavior which you will wish to cultivate are as follows:

- **"Do Without" To Grow Strong** - One of the envied attributes of the Stoics is their ability to persevere. Rich or poor, it is the same. This is because the Stoic will make it their practice to deny themselves things that many take for granted in life. This prepares them for those times in life when such things have been taken away. There are many ways you can do this. Eat simply for a week and avoid junk food, for instance. Turn off the air conditioner and use a fan or simply open the windows. Denying yourself of things you have come to expect from life will make you stronger. This is also known as "voluntary discomfort". It is a good principle to start mastering as it will teach you to be happy with what you have.

- **Recognize The "Good" In The "Bad"** - For the Stoic, there is no bad. For example, dangerous weather such as a hurricane or tornado may devastate an island. While this is lamentable, this is the work of nature, and as such, it is not good or bad – only nature. With a practical life application, this view is compelling as well. Did you lose your job? You have the opportunity to learn patience as you look for a new one. You have a chance to get a better job. This is heavily based on the Stoic belief that perception of a thing decides how much we are influenced by a thing. Nothing can hurt you without you giving it that power -- by the way you perceive something.

- **Accept Death Rather Than Fear It** - Death is natural and it is the great equalizer.

Marcus Aurelius once commented on this, stating that Alexander the Great and his horses' Groom were the same in death. Dispersed to their atoms [2]. Think of it as a perception hack. Instead of viewing yourself as the center of the universe, by realizing that our existence is temporary (at best), you are empowered in knowing this: There is no need to stress yourself trying to build a legacy or enslave yourself to fads or unrealistic expectations and achievements. The only important thing is to live true to our natures.

- **"View It From Above"** - Also known as "Plato's view", whenever you feel overwhelmed, take a birds-eye view of the world and your place within it. When "viewed from above", you can see the bigger picture. This allows us to see how insignificant many of life's challenges truly are in the scope of things.

- **Understand What You Can Influence And Control** - This is paramount. Once you understand instinctually what you can and cannot change, then the things you cannot change will lose their power to harm you. You choose what impressions you will infer from them. There is no "bad", only opportunity. Marcus Aurelius said it nicely, "The hindrance becomes the way." A Stoic is only concerned with what they may influence and control; anything else is a worthless distraction.

- **Be Greedy With Your Own Time** - People covet wealth and power easily, yet they seldom learn to covet the one thing that is most important-- time. Seneca speaks of this in his treatise "On the shortness of life". Rather than treating our time with the respect it deserves, most would spend it in revelry or useless binge-watching of reruns of their favorite shows. Sit back and think about that. Time is the most precious thing that you have.

Lastly, we would recommend that you not tell people that you are practicing Stoicism. Instead, let it be shown in your actions. Epictetus encouraged this, stating that just as sheep don't show the shepherds how much grass they have consumed, but rather express it in the fine wool that they produce, so you should do the same. If people take your silence as ignorance and it doesn't bother you, well, that's the first sign that you are becoming a philosopher! [3] Once you have digested the Stoic techniques, people will notice the changes anyway.

While these are some examples of what it means to be Stoic, there is certainly more to it. Together we will discuss these topics and more so that you can incorporate the Stoic principles into your life, starting with the core of Stoicism: Learning to recognize, at a glance, the things which you can control and the things which you cannot. This is the first step towards the happiness that Stoicism

WILL provide you.

Chapter 2 Do The Triage In Life

A Stoic learns that the things which they cannot control are unimportant. A distraction at best or a hindrance at the worst. As such, they learn to ignore these things. This is important to you because, properly practiced, mastery of this technique can lift the weight of the world off of your shoulders.

Worrying about things that you cannot control is pointless. It drains your energy and your time which you could be using in attacking the problems that you CAN solve.

In every situation, you need to ask yourself, "Is this within my control?" Let's discuss some examples so that you can get a better idea of what this means.

- **Someone Doesn't Like You Or Criticizes You** - Just as you have your own will and interpretations of things, so do others. Rather than view it as a rejection of you, accept that another's opinion is simply their own way of interpreting the world. It is your interpretation of a thing that hurts you, so why not view this person's behavior as simply a case of a person following their own nature? Epictetus espouses this view in the Discourses, urging us to treat our critics with compassion, telling ourselves that "He did what he believed was right." [4]. If you can do this, then opinions and criticism will roll off you like water off a duck's back.

- **You Have An Illness** - People get sick. It's not something that you can control. Some of us have to live with chronic conditions, for instance. Yes, this means that there are changes to your routine, but this is not something that you can change, so you should not waste energy focusing on it. Take what medications you need and go about your day. Epictetus even tells us of Agrippinus [5], a philosopher who used to praise all difficulties for the learning experiences which they brought (he'd even write songs praising his fevers when he had them!). The lesson here is to accept nature and work your will in whatever ways you choose.

- **Your Flight Is Delayed By A Snowstorm** - A lighter example but certainly viable for those of us who have a temper. You can't change the weather, and no amount of yelling at some poor airline employee is going to help. Accept delays like this as inevitable and focus on what you CAN change, like how you spend this unexpected gift of time.

- **Loss Of A Loved One** - While one of the most difficult things to accept, this is completely natural. Everything that lives will die. Rejoice that you were fortunate enough to share a part of their journey through life. Say your goodbyes at the funeral. Let this be enough because life is for the living, and death is truly something that you cannot change. Epictetus tells us that the best way to accomplish this is not to say "I lost something", but rather that "it was returned". Everything is experienced but briefly, and we don't own anything but our will and decisions. Even our bodies must go back to whence they came. You did not truly lose this person because you cannot own them. They were "loaned" to you, and the time came when they must be "returned". [6]

- **Physical Characteristics** - Too tall? Too short? Physical characteristics that we were born with cannot be changed (with some surgical exceptions). Dwelling on them is an exercise in futility. Express yourself in what you do, not how you look.

- **You Are Laid Off From A Job** - This happens. You cannot change the fact and dwelling on this fact takes away energy which you could be putting towards getting a new, maybe even better job!

These are but a few examples of things that you cannot change. It's rather like the "Serenity Prayer" (and it is plausible that the inspiration for writing it came from Stoicism):

"God, grant me the serenity to accept the things I cannot change,

Courage to change the things I can,

And wisdom to know the difference."

The message is the same, but Stoicism is a philosophy, not a religion, and we must learn to recognize these things for ourselves. Let's follow our examples of "things that you cannot change" with a few examples of things that you CAN change:

- **How You Spend Your "Free Time"** - Do you have a nagging feeling that your time could be better spent? You should listen to this. Write things. Journal your thoughts and experience. Learn new things. Always keep busy; after all, no amount of money in this world can buy you so much as an additional minute of your time.

- **The Type Of People That You Consort With** - Surround yourself with fellow thinkers. The company that you keep greatly influences your own behavior. Epictetus warns against this in the Discourses, stating that if your friends are dirty that it doesn't matter how clean you are, you will become a little dirty as well. [7]

- **The Amount Of Alcohol You Consume** - Barring alcoholism (which is more of a nature factor), you can decide how much you imbibe, and it is important that you do. Stoics prize their faculty of rational thought and alcohol. Well, it's not so conducive to that. Practice abstinence or moderation because, in this, you have the power to decide the strength of your reasoning.

- **How Many Luxuries You Allow In Life** - Denying yourself some of life's luxuries by practice is the way that a Stoic strengthens their resolve. This is done constantly as an affirmation of life. Should they lose these luxuries, the Stoic is nonplussed. They already know exactly what it means to lose these things and that they cannot only endure, but thrive in their absence.

This last example of "luxuries" is one that is worth a deeper look. Mastery of this technique can teach you to truly be happy with what you have, and this is a prize beyond measure. Let's discuss!

Chapter 3 Practice Voluntarily Discomfort

A Stoic must practice self-control and discipline. In "Letters to a Stoic", a passage from Seneca begins *"I shall give you also a lesson: Set aside a certain number of days, during which you shall be content with the scantiest and cheapest fare..."* [8] in which he advises the Stoics to live as if exceedingly poor. The purpose was so that it could be experienced, and the practitioner could ask, "Is this what I was afraid of?".

This is pure wisdom. Not only does voluntary discomfort prepare you for the worst, but it also teaches you to appreciate what you have. This gives you a way to deal properly with anxiety and fear. In a way, you are inoculating yourself against it. So, does one have to live like a pauper for a space to do this? Not necessarily. There are a number of small exercises that you can do for now. This will help you to work your way up to the larger sorts of sacrifice.

You are becoming stronger each time.

Let's discuss some practical examples:

- Spend a day with no air conditioner or heater.
- No meat for a day
- If you have social anxiety, spark up a conversation with a stranger.
- Leave a portion of each meal untouched for a day
- No beverages but water for a day

These are just some basic examples, but you get the idea. During your abstinence, you should meditate on the thought that your fate can give and take anything. Nothing is truly yours, but your will and judgment, everything else is given to you on "loan". As you work your way up with some of the smaller sacrifices, try moving up from one day to one week.

For instance:

- Spend one week without the heater or the air conditioner. You can do completely without or make do with a small fan or a space heater (provided that these are very basic.)
- Eat no meat for a week
- If you have social anxiety, volunteer somewhere for a week working with people.
- Eat smaller portions of food for one week.
- No beverages but water for one week

Voluntary discomfort is a powerful tool for a Stoic. We are all afraid, deep down, that should we lose everything that we might also lose ourselves. By forcing ourselves to experience what this is like, then we inure ourselves to the effects.

Facing your fears is a sure way to build self-discipline and character, so you will want to practice this often.

Some other exercises that you can use to toughen yourself up include:

- **Cold Showers** - What if you didn't have hot water, could you endure? Find out!

- **Sleeping On The Floor** - Beds are nice but taken for granted. Spend a week sleeping on the floor.

- **Morning Exercise** - If your job doesn't require a lot of physical labor, an exercise routine can show you what you are missing.

- **Journaling Your Thoughts** - If you are not used to writing down your thoughts, then an excellent exercise is writing them daily for a week. Entries don't have to take up a page or more, but don't limit yourself to one sentence a day.

- **Fasting** - Bread and water or simply water fasting for a day can be enlightening. Fasting has many benefits when done for longer periods as well, but you will want to consult your physician before fasting for any extended periods.

- **Give Yourself Less Sleep** - Spend a week sleeping less. If you normally sleep for 10 hours, then move to 8. If you normally sleep 8 hours, try functioning on 6. Sleep is one of the easiest things to learn to appreciate properly!

Exercises such as these are designed to challenge your ideas of comfort. They will teach you how many things you take for granted and rely upon. Further, they will show you that many of these "creature-comforts" are unnecessary. A Stoic finds happiness in their self-discipline and their control over the things which they may influence.

By learning not to let your happiness be decided by how many things you have or do not have, then these things lose their power over you.

In his "Discourses", Epictetus tells us that the things that we let ourselves desire become our masters. Not only the things, even, but that whoever controls the things that we desire becomes our master. By constantly challenging yourself to do without, you will gradually lessen the power which these "mere possessions" hold on you [9].

A Stoic must recognize that comforts and possessions are ephemeral. These are things that you can live without. Further, possessions do not confer status. Epictetus states [10] that when a person tells you that they are better than you because they are wealthy or a better speaker, for instance, that this is simply not true.

The more logical assessment of the Stoic would be, "You have more wealth than I do. Therefore, your wealth is superior to mine." or "You are a better public speaker. Therefore, your oratory skills are superior."

A man or woman is not wealth, oratory skills, or possessions. Recognize this by denying yourself comforts and ascribing value only to your reasoning. Value your judgment. Treasure your ability to manipulate the things which you can change and to ignore the things that you cannot affect. This is the wisdom of the Stoic.

How we are perceived is a subject of stress and consternation for most of us. Yet it is only a simple matter of the impression which we choose to take from such critiques. In the next chapter, we'll tackle how a Stoic deals with an insult.

Chapter 4 Deal With The Insults

There is always going to be someone who will try to provoke you. Some people enjoy it. Others simply do not have control over their tempers, which you have or are currently developing. So, how does a Stoic deal with critics or insults?

Seneca had some practical advice on the subject in his essay "Anger, Mercy, and Revenge". In it, he says: *"The one who has harmed you is either stronger or weaker than you: if he's weaker, give him a break; if he's stronger, give yourself a break."* [11]

This advice is certainly practical. What about the anger that forces you to feel? To this, we need to remember that a Stoic decides how they wish to feel. Epictetus says to us that if someone hits us or insults us with the intent of harm that we must believe that they have harmed us for it to be effective.

If we allow ourselves to be provoked, then we are complicit in the provocation. Basically, if you let someone "push your buttons" and let yourself be angry about it, then you helped them in provoking yourself. [12]

A Stoic analyzes everything. So, instead of flying off the handle at every insult, why not try this? First, promise yourself that you will not respond immediately. This is a good habit for a Stoic to be in with any situation.

You control your own happiness, and no one can take it from you without your permission.

You control your judgment.

So now that you have taken a moment to distance

yourself from this harmless collection of words which someone thinks they can provoke you with, what should you do?

There are many good responses. You could make your own joke about yourself, for instance. Self-deprecating humor is a means of disarming one who would provoke us with words, especially if your own insult to yourself is funnier. If someone calls you fat, smile and move away from them, saying, "I'll just relocate so that I'm not blocking all of your sunlight." with a smile and a slight, gracious bow.

By not allowing them to provoke you and by making light of yourself, in turn, you show someone the worth of their paltry words, and more importantly, everyone will see that this person does not possess the wit or the strength to move you in the slightest. Socrates deflected insult with humor sometimes.

In one famous example, it was said that when someone came looking for a philosopher and did not recognize him, rather than take insult, he would escort them to talk to some other philosophers that he knew — usually his friends, namely Protagoras or Hippias. Instead of taking offense, he smiled and treated the request as if he was simply telling someone how to find cabbage in a grocery store. [13]

What would it have served him, after all, to be angry over something as simple as ignorance? Socrates was always happy to state that he knew nothing except that he knew nothing, and we can all learn a thing or two from this example.

If self-deprecating humor is not your style, why not employ an analysis of what was said? First, is it truly an insult, or is it a critique? When someone is critical of us, it is very easy to take it personally.

A Stoic is taught to behave differently, however. If someone criticizes you, then you should take it one of two ways.

First, ask yourself if the criticism is valid. If it is, don't meet this with anger. This person has just advised you on something that you can improve.

Even if the criticism was delivered by the most mean-spirited, nasty person that you know, if the criticism is correct and you feel injured, then you are truly angry at yourself. Don't be.

Take the criticism constructively and improve yourself. Don't waste your energy being angry with the "child" who brought it to your attention.

Further, if the criticism is wrong, would you give it power by accepting it as an insult? Epictetus tells us that when someone criticizes us incorrectly, they are the ones who suffer for being incorrect. He advises that you treat them with compassion, like an ignorant child who is only doing and saying what they think is right. [14]

Another choice that you have with insults is simply ignoring them. Epictetus states in his Discourses that you should stand in front of a rock and throw your best insults at it. How powerful are those words now? Be like the rock and no one can ever hurt you with insults.

A Stoic is only concerned with the things that he or she can change, and as an adult, you know how hard it is to change another person's opinion about anything.

Let them have their ignorance.

So, what did Marcus Aurelius have to say on the subject? The wise emperor reminds us that a Stoic is only concerned with what belongs to himself (logic, judgment, impressions we choose to take) and that such a person is thus impervious to insults. This person should also be wary also of valuing praise that comes from the same unbalanced people. After all, why should you value praise that comes from one who is not even satisfied with themselves?

We have advised what to do with direct insults and criticisms of the self. So, what about rumors? People love to seed them, and as often as not, the rumor comes to your attention from a friend or other curious innocent who wishes to know, "is it true?"

Epictetus had a fine response for this, further arguing that humor is the best way to diffuse the harm in incorrect words. He says you shouldn't try to defend yourself but rather state, *"Yes, and they don't know the half of it, or they could have said more!"* [15]

Insults have no power over you. Respond by insulting yourself to show that you are self-aware. Take criticisms as lessons where you can improve yourself. Don't play their game. Anger is an affront to your tranquility and happiness and not worth your time. Why care what THEY think? You can only control what YOU think.

Chapter 5 Simplifying Lifestyle

Do you always have to have the most expensive clothing? Do you find it shameful to take the bus instead of driving a new car to work?

Why?

Are you your clothing? Are you your car? Of course not. Shame is an external influence that we allow into our lives, letting it damage our tranquility. Like an insult, there is only power in shame if you allow it to touch you.

A Stoic should be humble and happy for the things that they have. Let's go into our first examples, clothing and the bus.

If you always wear expensive clothing, why is this?

Are you trying to impress someone with your wealth? With your taste? Is it a specific someone?

A Stoic will analyze their thoughts to get to the root of an issue, and you will need to get in the habit of doing this as well.

Wealth and clothing are not ours. They are on "loan" to us and can be taken away at any time. By putting your self-worth into these things, then you are risking losing it the moment that they are gone. Is it worth that risk simply to impress others (when the only thing that you can truly own is what YOU think?).

What about riding the bus? That car is a status symbol. It represents wealth or independence. So does a car make you free, or is it just a visible representation that you keep to impress others? If it is cheaper to ride the bus (rather than pay for gas and maintenance on the car), why not take the bus?

Sure, it takes longer and your time is precious. Could you not counter this by using your time wisely? You can read on the bus. You can practice a new language with lessons on your phone or an mp3 player. You can enjoy the scenery as it passes by. It is all up to you.

Becoming immune to shame and humbling yourself is an important step in becoming a Stoic. By expressing who you are in your actions, rather than your possessions, you set an example that others cannot help but notice. Some will even wish to emulate you. Epictetus said it best when he advised that one should not pride themselves on any assets that they did not truly own.

If you have a beautiful, sporty car, are the traits of the car yours? Of course not. Why would you brag or take credit for its traits [16], this thing which anyone could buy if they had the money? The only thing that truly belongs to you is the impressions that you decide to take from the world around you.

If you should wish to take pride in this, then, by all means, do so because your thoughts and the impressions that you take are truly and uniquely your own.

Simplify your lifestyle, appreciate what you have, and accept that your wealth and possessions are not you and are not even really yours. This is the way of the Stoic.

Chapter 6 View From Above

Also known as "Plato's view", to view from above is to take a moment where you stop and try to realize the bigger picture.

For instance, someone at your work irritates you. Rather than taking offense, you start thinking about how many other people there are at the office, working on specific things that further contribute to one goal.

Take a step further, view these people as part of a company. An entity composed of all these people working towards whatever commodity it is that the company provides. Is that all that the company does? Not at all. It also provides work for a percentage of people in the city.

How important is it in the scheme of things? This is an important view to understand. When you break things down, then personal problems become almost laughable to your Stoic sensibilities. Everyone and everything are just a tiny cog in a great and powerful machine.

Does this mean that we are helpless? Not at all. You control your thoughts and impressions. You control your behavior.

Taking a larger view can show you that your employment is simply that — a means to an end. Allowing yourself to be angry is a slight to yourself.

That wise, Stoic emperor Marcus Aurelius advised us that seeing things from above puts everything in a new perspective. "Luxuries, power, war... all the worries of everyday life are suddenly ridiculous." [17]

This is a powerful lesson that gives the Stoic a view of "global consciousness". Why should you worry so much about these external things? The clothing and the cars that are popular in your country might be laughable or shameful in another.

The attitude a coworker is showing you might be normal behavior in a city across the globe, where aggressive honesty is lauded or unfiltered communication is encouraged.

This is another example where the Stoic learns that all-powerful lesson of what he or she can and cannot control. Once you take this to heart and allow yourself to see the bigger picture, then you will know what you can ignore (or at least pay minimal attention to, but only in how it affects you.).

Remember, the Stoic is only concerned with the

things which they can change. So, when you are feeling overwhelmed, be sure to step back for a moment and view the world as a bird might.

Realize that there is genuinely very little that you can actually control and that, because of this, you SHOULD exercise control on everything that it is within your power to do so with.

You can't change the world, but you can change yourself. Practice the Stoic ideals so that no insult can harm you, no possessions can enslave you, and so that nothing can take away the happiness which you allow yourself to have.

Chapter 7 Cognitive Distancing

Some people like to compare Stoics to the "Vulcans" from the television show "Star Trek". This is because a Stoic often appears to show little emotion. So, does a Stoic really not feel anything?

Of course not.

A Stoic simply trains themselves to recognize what they can and cannot control. A human cannot completely control their emotions like a fictional alien race. So, what is one to do?

Well, as a Stoic values their ability to control what can be controlled, then the first step is cognitive distancing.

Simply put, step back from the emotion for a

moment. This is something that you can practice, starting small and then moving your way up.

For example -- let's say that on your way to work you pick up a newspaper from a coin-operated machine. You pull out your paper and part of it rips, just as the spring-loaded door slams home to prevent you from grabbing an undamaged paper.

Your first and most honest reaction is to curse, is it not?

So why are you cursing? Are you angry at the person who made the machine? Are you angry that the person in charge of maintaining the machine is blissfully unaware that the newspapers can get snagged in it? Perhaps you are simply angry that the paper is ripped, but the paper itself is an inanimate object. Why yell at something that can't feel your anger (much less actually provoke it).

What you need to realize is that this anger only has power because you allowed it. What happened is entirely external. You're angry, but rather than getting another paper or reading the story online, will you let it color your day?

You can't control what happened, but you CAN control the impression you draw. This is something that we often repeat because this is the hardest lesson to learn.

Another excellent example of cognitive distancing is this. Say you are at work where a lot of email communication is standard. A coworker has made you angry by suggesting that you aren't pulling your own weight or perhaps they have put off work which they were responsible for and it's holding everything up.

Do you write an email, maybe even copying it to

your boss, while you are angry?

We don't recommend it.

Take the Stoic approach instead with this little exercise. Write the email and save it as a draft. Next, wait one day to send it (or until after lunch if it absolutely cannot wait). By writing it and putting it aside, you are giving yourself a lesson in how much emotion clouds your judgment if you allow it to.

After lunch or better, the next day, read your email and remove all traces of emotion from it. You will have a lot to delete. This is because intense emotion can blind us and affect our judgment. If you would have sent out that email, everyone who is not experiencing your consternation will nonetheless be well aware of it.

Words written in haste and emotion look like what they are.

Once you've tried this and seen for yourself, add it to your daily life and try to expand on it. After all, is it wiser to act immediately when you are angry and want to get something done, or is it better to approach any issue with as much control as you can muster?

We aren't saying that you can always control your emotions. Stoics are human just like everyone else, and you will make a lot of mistakes on your path as a philosopher. If you keep exercising your judgment, however, then these mistakes will slowly become less and less as you learn to own your own judgment and, therefore, your own happiness.

Another good exercise that you can use to strengthen your response to fiery emotions is this.

Get yourself a notebook, and for one week, write down every time that you get angry. Let the moment pass, and when you are alone, write down what made you angry or to feel anxious, close the notebook, and continue on your week.

On Sunday (or whatever day you are off work and relaxed), read your list. What do you feel you should have done about these things that made you angry or that scared you? Cause a scene? Snipe at a coworker? Would that lead to a better working environment? Likely these things that blinded you for a moment are painfully clear at this distance.

This is an important realization and the beginning of very deep and very Stoic wisdom.

Stepping aside from these violent emotions, we learn what such knee-jerk reactions will truly get us. As a Stoic, it is your duty to understand this and to remind yourself constantly.

Don't worry; it gets easier with time. Other simple exercises that can help:

- Count to 5 or 10 before responding when your emotions flare.
- Consider why you are angry or scared rather than simply venting your anger or running from something.
- Say to yourself, "This emotion moves me because I'm allowing it." and let it pass. Go somewhere quiet if you need to.

Epictetus states that people who are possessed of strong constitutions can tolerate extremes of hot or cold weather with relative ease. The same is true of people who possess strong mental health due to practice and conditioning, as they can handle grief, joy, anger, and other emotions that vex those who do not often enough exercise their control. [18]

Use your growing Stoic powers of judgment so that you may delay emotional judgments long enough to see what they are and whether or not acting on them serves you. This is easier for some than others. If it is harder for you, then try this. If you cannot stop the emotion, delay it. If you cannot delay it, force yourself to be silent rather than speaking it.

Every moment that you exercise control over an emotion successfully is a step further towards absolute control over it.

Now consider how much control you might possess after years of this practice?

Chapter 8 Empathetic Understanding

In chapter 42 of "Discourses", we are told the importance of Empathy as it relates to the Stoics' ability to ignore criticism and the actions of others when they attempt to wrong us.

The technique and its reasoning are sound, and the essence of it is this: Other people cannot possibly be guided by our own views. They can only base their actions on their own. As such, if their views are wrong, do they not suffer the indignity of being misguided?

A Stoic is taught to empathize with this person rather than to seek a quarrel. It is enough to say to yourself, "This person is only doing what they feel is right, based on their views of the world.". [19]

Just as you cannot own anything but your own views and judgments, it must be realized that others, even those who judge you poorly, are only practicing the same right. Rather than "strike back" when someone attempts to malign you with words, you should attempt to understand what is really occurring.

Is it not sad that someone would waste so much energy in an attempt to discredit you?

Take a moment to analyze their behavior.

This person has decided to base their actions on an unproven assumption and, worse, to attempt to convince others and themselves that this assumption is valid (to hurt you in some cases, in others to make themselves feel important). By this logic, they are basing their self-importance on their ability to debase YOU.

What an unhappy existence. Unlike the Stoic, they are attempting to own what cannot be owned. The views of others. Your view.

Rather than take offense, it is more realistic to feel pity. For a Stoic, their criticism should be interpreted only in one of two ways:

- **As A Valid Criticism** - in which case we should be thankful to them for addressing a flaw in our own logic or behavior. If this is something we can control, then it is in our power to change, so the one delivering criticism has done us a favor.

- **As A Flawed Criticism** - If the criticism is about something which we cannot control, for instance, "you are old and I am young", then why should it matter to you? This is not something you can change. If you allow yourself to be angry, then you are not exercising Stoic control. Why not smile and say, "Then you move faster while I have seen and learned many things, are we not both truly lucky."?

Never forget that as a Stoic, you are the one who decides what impressions you take from something. Someone cannot drive you to anger without your first allowing it. Your happiness belongs to you. If someone seeks to harm you with their words, then they are making the mistake of basing their happiness on something outside of their control.

They deserve your pity.

Socrates said it best. Whenever someone would insist on him, "I have insulted you.", he would answer with a smile and the words, "A lot of good may it do you!" [20]

Chapter 9 Show Up Every Day

A Stoic must be committed to pushing themselves. You need to exercise your control. If something is within your influence, you must OWN it. Chapter 51 of Discourses [21] addresses this with a compelling argument. It asks, "How long will you wait before you decide to demand the best of yourself?"

So, how long?

You've been given the precepts of Stoicism. The seeds are planted. Should you not now strive to ensure that they grow? As you are an adult now, your time is less, and if you procrastinate constantly, you could die without achieving enlightenment. Stoicism hasn't changed in its validity, only in your failure to exercise it.

You will have failed because you chose to fail.

Don't let this happen! Rather, accept that every day is important. A Stoic knows that death is natural and that everything is merely loaned to us, even our own bodies. With this in mind, you must choose to PROGRESS.

Since you cannot know how long you have, you should live as if everything depends on the events of this single day.

Further, do not look for help or harm in others. A Stoic must look for these things in themselves. We own nothing but our impressions and our happiness, and no one is going to get these things for you. After all, how could they? Like you, they can only own their own happiness.

Your self-discipline is like a muscle. At first, it is weak, but when you exercise daily, it slowly increases in mass and power. If your self-discipline needs a little work, then start slow. Some examples:

1. Always arrive at work 20 minutes early. The work is not as important as the intent. This gives you time to read the news, have a cup of coffee, or just to have some breathing space before you "leap into the fray". It is a discipline, and others will notice when you exercise it.

   Some ways to gain time in the morning are as follows:
   a. Shower the night before
   b. Iron and lay out your clothes the night before
   c. Set your current alarm 30 minutes earlier than usual

2. Exercise briefly every morning. You won't want to, at first, but it is a way to start your day by asserting your control. It will make your

body stronger at the same time as it strengthens your mind.

3. If you are feeling physically weak or overwhelmed by emotion, take a cold shower. It's a useful exercise. It demonstrates your will to push past obstacles at the same time that it reminds you to appreciate simple things like heated water.

4. Make a list of small things that need to be done that you have been putting off. Pick one thing off of that list each day and DO IT. It doesn't matter how small it seems. Doing something, anything, is better than doing nothing, and in time you will find that the tasks which you are assigning yourself are becoming more substantial. The small tasks are like a grain of sand in an oyster that grows into a pearl.

Show up every day. In every intent and interaction, ask yourself, "Is this within my control?" and if it is, then do something useful with it.

A Stoic owns their own happiness.

Chapter 10 Never Play The Victim

Attitude is everything. It is worthless to spend your time complaining about things that you cannot change. So, how do we do this?

By reinforcing our intent to ignore the things that we cannot change.

Why would you complain about something that you cannot change? It serves no purpose but to drain you of energy.

In Book 5 of Marcus Aurelius' "Meditations", we are given a persuasive lesson [22]. We'll paraphrase it here. Aurelius says that when we wake up, we should affirm to ourselves that "I am waking up to do the work of a human being." Why should we be dissatisfied, he argues, when we are doing the work for which we were explicitly designed? Why should we lay in bed all day? "Well, it's comfortable.", one might argue, to which we are then to ask, "Am I here only to experience pleasure but never to exert any action or hard work?"

This is an excellent question.

Aurelius continues to ask us if we see the other inhabitants of the world around us neglecting to do their parts. The plants that we see, the birds, indeed, all of nature around us, do we see any laziness there?

Plants give us oxygen, sometimes food too. Birds help distribute seeds. Bees help to pollinate plants. What about man? Yes, we need rest, but Nature has set limits to how much we need. The same goes for eating and drinking. Yet most of us can gladly ignore these limits and indulge, until it comes time for us to act, to be productive. Thus, we fall short of what we might achieve.

If you agree with this, then ask yourself further: What of the ones who love their arts and actions? How many artists spend countless hours perfecting a brushstroke, skipping baths and meals. What of the architect who can't stop putting in extra hours at work and even reads architectural journals in the bathroom? We all know at least one expert in a particular field who has found their niche and channels their energy into it.

Do you love yourself less?

Yes, there are situations we are thrust into, which we cannot change. What you can change is your attitude about it. Find your place in society. It doesn't have to be lofty. Remember that the Stoic takes the "view from above" and take a step back from things.

Realize how little that you control so that you can take the reins on the things that you CAN. Here are some practical examples:

- If you work around people who complain a lot, instead of letting it drain your morale, try instead to make a mental note of which complaints are within the complainer's power to change. Keep this to yourself; your turn is next.

- Keep a notepad handy, and when you catch yourself complaining about something that you cannot change, write it down. Review it at the end of each week and see if you can teach yourself to start ignoring these things until your list is blank.

- Assert each morning, "I am responsible for my own happiness because nothing can harm me if I do not allow it to."

When a Stoic has taught themselves to recognize

the things that they can change and to ignore the things which they cannot, then they can never be a "victim".

Chapter 11 Practice Delayed Gratification

The way of the Stoic involves a lot of discipline. We are taught that anyone who controls the things that we value is essentially our master; thus, a Stoic must learn not to covet things if they would master themselves.

This is extremely difficult to do, but delayed gratification is an excellent first step. By acknowledging temptation but delaying our gratification from it, then we slowly take away the power of a "thing" to hold us captive.

Why is this so important? Is it wrong to want money or a fancy car? Of course not. What is wrong is needing these things to define to yourself or to others who you are. You aren't money. You are not your car, your house, or your job. That doesn't mean that we don't have temptations, however.

Aside from the lofty ones, some simple ones can get us all the time. Have you ever stopped a project to catch the latest episode of a favorite show? Have you ever spent a weekend recovering from a night out with the boys or girls? Many things can make us less productive. The first step in taking away their power to control you is to exercise a little control of your own.

Let's give a practical example. You have a work project that is taking most of your time, and you have been invited to go out in the middle of the week. You KNOW that it is going to affect your productivity, but you also feel that you deserve a reward for your hard work.

What to do? Well, let's analyze it. Do you take pride in your work? If so, is it worth it to you to do work of lesser quality for the remaining days of the week (or even for a single day, because you will have less energy the next day if you stay up late even if you recover quickly)? Lastly, could you not instead celebrate the finished project on Friday night, when it would only impact your weekend?

What serves you better? In an ideal scenario, a Stoic might not be tempted to go out at all, as clarity of thought is highly prized, but this is something that everyone has to work up to. By taking a temptation (going out Wednesday night) and applying a measure of control to it (no, I'll go out Friday night!), you are exercising your will. You also accomplish getting the fun that you would have enjoyed that Wednesday while still keeping your work integrity intact.

As a challenge to yourself, we propose an exercise. If you have one temptation that you indulge in regularly every week, then we would like you to reschedule it. Defer it by a week, a day, or even a few hours and do this for a month. At the end of this month, you should contemplate the results of this experiment.

Did you lose anything by exercising your control? Even better, did you gain anything?

By deferring your gratification, you will lessen the power of the things that enslave you. Even better, as you learn not to expect an immediate reward for your work, you will empower yourself to push through the roadblocks that keep you from longer-term goals!

Chapter 12 Ignore Naysayers

While some criticism is honest (if not always delivered tactfully), there are some people who actually thrive in the act of delivering it. This should be watched so that you can deliver them their just desserts.

By ignoring them.

Modern naysayers, often known as "Trolls", just like to get a rise out of you. As a Stoic, you will learn to recognize them very quickly. So, why is ignoring them the best course? For one, a Stoic knows that the criticism of another is either instructive to us or a result of another's faulty logic.

A troll, however, doesn't even deserve that consideration. When the number of criticisms is constant, varied, and for no apparent reason, then listening to it only gives them power.

Do you really care what a stranger thinks? Why is it so crucial to them to vocalize opinions specifically about you? It is important to notice this kind of unhealthy attention and to remind yourself that it is not under your control. Avoid them if you can. If you cannot, then ignoring them is the best.

While it might be tempting to engage them with some criticisms of your own, you must resist this temptation. A Stoic has no interest in what they cannot control. Besides, what are you worried about? If the criticisms have no basis in fact, then they don't matter.

No one will think ill of you for refusing to play the fool's game. Rather, play your own by holding your tongue.

While the criticisms may sting at first, it gets easier to ignore this type of person with practice. There is also another good reason to adopt this attitude. Acknowledging this type of person only accomplishes the following:

- People wonder if the criticisms are valid
- People associate you with your company, and you are spending a lot of time with this fool
- You end up wasting valuable time on something that you cannot change or control

On the flip side, ignoring this type of person empowers you. It shows that your time is important and that you are secure in your own strengths and weaknesses. It also demonstrates, by your actions, that you do not suffer fools.

While self-deprecating humor can get the job done, we would challenge you to try simply ignoring the offender. Try it for a month and see what happens. While it is definitely a challenge (holding your tongue while some annoying friend or coworker keeps rattling off faux-faults that they seem to find in you), consider this: what must this person see in the mirror that makes them so determined to focus on anything and everybody else?

There is no need to stoop to provocation when pity is obviously called for.

By whatever means, you must reserve your time only for the factors in life that you can control or change. After all, a Stoic demonstrates their worth in actions, not merely in words.

Chapter 13 Do Less

It's a deceptive title for a chapter, no? We are not talking about doing less work, of course (hey, we're Stoics!), but rather that one should focus on a small number of things rather than spreading oneself thin with too many.

It sounds like an easy thing to do, but you might be surprised. In this modern information age, we often tout the value of multitasking.

Is this really a good thing?

Yes, multitasking can be useful, but it is not necessarily always the best approach. So how do you decide how you approach something?

By eliminating that which is superfluous and planning in advance.

In chapter 29 of Discourses [23], there is actually direct advice on planning out a task. We are told that we should reflect not only on what the plan will initially require but on each stage to follow before even deciding to take up the task. By doing this, we don't set ourselves up for failure or frustration during the more difficult phases of the task because we have already broken it down into its components.

How, then, does one decide what is superfluous? The easiest means to do this is to ask yourself this: "Is what I am doing now connected to my task?".

If it is not, then is it something that you can do later?

You must learn to focus!

Start by breaking your task down into a series of smaller tasks. Note the most important tasks, as well. You can seldom go wrong by accomplishing as many of these in advance as possible.

Another way to "do less to do more" is through the grouping of like tasks. Examples might include:

- If you need to call one person on a specific day, make any other necessary phone calls for your task at the same time

- If you need to pick up a supply item at one location, if you can get more supplies in advance there or if other supplies can be purchased nearby, save a trip and do it all at once

- If an aspect of your project involves the computer (like making a spreadsheet for your finances), then this is also a good time to take care of any emails related to the project as well

Remember that as a Stoic, your time is precious

and by planning well, you can save quite a lot of it while performing your task more efficiently. The ability to break down tasks into their component parts and to prioritize and group these components will also teach you how to achieve your goals realistically.

Breaking a task or a problem into smaller, more easily-digested bits is just another tool in the Stoic's toolbox. If you can accomplish all of the tasks that you have outlined, then the results are within your control, and that control is what Stoicism is all about.

Just be careful, there is very little that you cannot accomplish when you break those "impossible" tasks into smaller "merely difficult" ones!

Chapter 14 Be Grateful For Your Blessings

In chapter 3, we spoke of voluntary discomfort and one of the lessons that comes from this is the appreciation of the things that we have. There are so many things that we take for granted, such as centralized heating and air, microwave ovens, cellular phones, the list goes on and on. What would you do if you did not have these things? What if you didn't have a refrigerator, an oven, or even electricity?

You could choose to despair, but is this not an impression? A Stoic would not damage their happiness in this fashion. Rather, they would learn to appreciate fruits growing in nature. They might learn to cook delicious meals by a fire.

The warmth of the fire itself, would that not be a blessing?

Aurelius contemplates this in his "Meditations", advising us to not only appreciate the things around us but to appreciate the imperfections. [24] For instance, with freshly baked bread, there are cracks that occur naturally in the baking, ingredients that sometimes rise to the top and decorate it in a fashion... these were not intended by the baker but nonetheless made our mouths water when we see them. Even delicious fruits, rotting on the tree, become touched with colors that add to the beauty of the fruit even as their decay reduces them to an inedible state. If we should look, everywhere there are examples to bring pleasure and encourage contemplation and look we should! View everything around you with the same pleasure as the sculptor or the painter, feverishly striving to capture even an approximation of what's around all of us.

If we only choose to look.

We tend to tie our happiness to things, and this is dangerous. Our consumer-driven society leads to competition with our friends and neighbors for the latest gadgets or the shiniest jewelry. Get a phone call on your cell while you are at a restaurant? When you are answering it, people are judging you for your phone.

Some people take pleasure in noting that their television set is bigger than yours.

Drink tap water (which has higher cleanliness standards in some countries than it's more expensive bottled variety), and you'll get judged as well. Ultimately, it's ridiculous. Why should ANYONE subscribe to it?

As a Stoic, if you practice voluntary discomfort, then you will gain an appreciation for things that you take for granted at the same time that you will know that you could live without those things.

Negative visualization, which is simply a deep contemplation of how your life would be living in a 3rd world country or if you were homeless on your own, can also help you to cultivate a Stoic mindset.

Express yourself in your actions and in your examples rather than the things that you were able to collect with money. Your personal happiness and your enlightened opinions are the only things that you can truly own.

What else do we really need?

Some exercises which you can try to help express or increase your appreciation for the things which you have:

- Instead of going out, spend the night at home. Cook for yourself instead of ordering out and enjoy the night sky from the back yard.

- Take a week off sodas, replacing them with bottled water. This will reaffirm that something you take for granted is actually a luxury.

- Take cold showers every day for a week. Some people don't have the luxury of hot water. Could you survive without it?

There is much to be thankful for if you simply teach yourself how to look.

Chapter 15 You Can Live Happy Anywhere

Aside from ascribing one's happiness to the "number of toys that we die with", another common belief that binds us is "I would be happy if I only lived in _____."

Is this true?

Why?

As a Stoic, your happiness is up to you. Certain things in other places might be pleasing. If you lived in Texas, you could have a pecan tree in your yard. If you lived in some places in California then maybe you could walk to the beach when you liked. If you lived in New York, you could have a "real" slice of deep-dish pizza pie.

All of these things are nice, but really, is your happiness contingent on these things? What if you lived in the woods in a log cabin next to a waterfall?

It's all ultimately scenery because a Stoic achieves their own happiness through their appreciation for the things they have and the impressions that they choose to take in life.

If you lived in Siberia, you could choose to bundle up and take up ice sculpting. If you lived in the desert just outside of Marrakesh with a solar panel on the top of your mud house, you could be happy and content with 2 hours of free electricity a day.

When you have learned to appreciate the things that you have and to ignore the things that you cannot control, the sky is the limit.

We should be very cautious about nostalgia, which is often the culprit when we find ourselves fondly missing a particular location. We develop strong ties to our roots, and there is nothing wrong with that, but we also tend to paint pictures in our memories, which become more of an ideal than the actual way that things happened.

Analyze your thoughts and try to determine what it is that you are actually missing. Was there something in the past that you remember so fondly that relates to a current goal? Is it because you know more now then you knew then?

If it is the former, you can use it, but the latter is out of your control. We cannot change the past.

Remember, when we allow our happiness to be reliant on people, places, or things, then we are setting ourselves up for disappointment. You cannot control what a person will do, nor guarantee that your childhood home has not changed, and possessions cannot define or truly fulfill you.

Aurelius has some excellent advice on this. [25] He states that we tend to purchase retreats for ourselves. Homes hidden deep in the woods or sitting in tranquility high in the mountains or perhaps sitting opposite of stunning seashores. Naturally, those who do not have one of these will desire them, but the Stoic emperor warns against this.

"It is the mark of the common man.", he says, because it is within the power of all to retire within themselves. There is no place in the world quieter or freer from trouble than inside one's own soul. There, a person can look upon their own thoughts and if those thoughts are of a certain caliber, then they will know a perfect tranquility.

A tranquility, he says, that is nothing more than the good ordering of your own mind.

Chapter 16 Help The Common Good And Maintain Social Relationships

While a lot of people envision the Stoic as the wise old man living alone on the mountain, this is actually a huge misconception. Stoics are taught to be active members of their community, serving the common good. In the "Fragments" portion of "Discourses", we are taught something about a phrase that you have probably heard.

"Know thyself."

Inscribed on the Temple of Apollo at Delphi until it was destroyed in 390 A.D., this maxim was one of the Delphic Maxims (a series of aphorisms said to have come from Apollo's oracle there). It sounds pretty straightforward; You should know yourself.

There is a little more to this, however.

In "Fragments", we are told that the way to know yourself is also to know the community in which you belong. If you are part of a group of chorus singers in your church or in an entertainment capacity, you should know these people you are surrounded with as well as how each contributes to the harmony that you produce together. For a soldier, part of knowing yourself is knowing the members of your company. It is understanding how you integrate. Everyone around us has an effect, from those we admire to the ones that we despise.

The Stoics see the world as one great community, ruled over by what they called "supreme providence". [29] This providence could be referred to by a number of names. Call it God, "the Gods", Fate, destiny, universal purpose, or even creative reason.

Our job as human beings is then to live in harmony with this universal purpose, accept and love our fates, and to stop ascribing value to those possessions and other aspects of life that can be taken away from us on a whim.

This is the path to inner peace, as long as we can keep ambition, greed, and reliance on luxuries at bay.

Being a part of the community, for a Stoic, involves giving back. It involves directing your actions for the benefit of the community. There are many ways that this can be done:

- **Voting** - Vote in your local community. You are part of it, and your voice should be heard.
- **Teaching A Skill** - Teaching a skill to a member of your community means that all can benefit from your knowledge. If you teach someone some carpentry basics, your

community benefits. Teach someone how to play music, and your community has more sweet music.

- **Learning A Skill** - Learn from other members of your community to strengthen both your knowledge and your bond with those around you.

- **Adding Members To The Community** - Starting a family empowers the community as a whole. Raising your children with good values helps the values of the community overall, as people learn by example.

- **"Random Acts Of Kindness"** - Kindness delivered to those in need, with no expectation of something in return, is an excellent way to aid your community. Do some volunteer work. Hire someone who is out of work to help you with a project. Feed homeless strangers. No one knows better than a Stoic that possessions come and go. While you cannot eliminate homelessness and hunger in the world, you can certainly lessen it within your own community.

It is in our nature to be social creatures. Think of the city in which you live as a smaller version of the universe-- a microcosm. By living according to your Stoic ideas and abiding by the local laws of the community of which you are part of you are yet making a contribution.

Does this mean that life will always be favorable? Of course not. People get sick and die. People lose their fortunes. You can live fairly and honorably and still find yourself in court sometime. If you do and the judge rules against you, as a Stoic and a member of the community, you should accept the decision. After all, the judge is also working for the community and their views are not under your control.

Be satisfied, because you did your part in answering to the community summons, just as the judge did by making a decision with the community welfare in mind. [30]

Know yourself by knowing and serving your community. When it comes to doing good for the community, keep in mind that you can be one of three types of givers:

- The type who gives a service or gift and marks it mentally, to call upon it later
- The type who gives and doesn't call it a "favor" but still feels that they are owed
- The type of person who simply gives and never thinks about it, like a vine or a tree that produces fruit [31]

Be like the vine, of course. Just as Stoicism has taught you that possessions can master you, the same teachings should also tell you that giving with the intent of mastering another is wrong. Just keep producing "fruit" like the vine and keeping to your principles, so that your community benefits not only by your labors but by your example.

Don't forget that you should not "announce" that you are a philosopher to this same community with your words, only with your actions. The goal of serving your community is simply that, to serve your community. Behaving otherwise is unbecoming of a philosopher.

A Stoic doesn't need to advertise.

Lastly, we would advise that while you should become closer to your community, be selective in the types of people with whom you surround yourself.

Remember that it is very easy to become like these people unless you can, through your actions and values, cause them to emulate you. Also, that if you consort with someone covered in dirt that you are bound to get dirty yourself! [33]

Know and serve your community that you may also know and serve yourself. It is your duty as a Stoic and a citizen.

Chapter 17 Accept And Appreciate Yourself

Accepting yourself is essential in Stoicism. You need to understand and accept your nature.

One important lesson from "Discourses" [26] states that we should not trouble ourselves with thoughts like "I'm going to live my life as a nobody, alone and unimportant."

This begs the question, is a lack of distinction bad?

How is this something that you can control? Can you invite yourself to the chic parties or give yourself that CEO job?

Of course not.

This is something that is out of your control, and therefore, there is no dishonor in a lack of distinction. What about being unimportant? Arguably, you are very important, the MOST important in the areas that are within your control. These areas where you are in control must be your source of self-worth.

A Stoic diligently takes control of everything that they can.

So, what about wealth? With wealth, you could spoil your friends and give nice things to your loved ones. The answer to this that Discourses provides is: "Show me a way that I can obtain such wealth without compromising my principles and I'll go and get it.".

As possessions tend to bind us, the Stoic recognizes that compromising your own principles for a handful of things that aren't so good for you in the first place is ridiculous. So, what about this "alone" part of the argument? Given a choice, would you want a rich, less-principled friend or a faithful friend with principles?

Stoicism is a difficult path in this regard, but it is undoubtedly a rewarding one.

What of the views of others and how they relate to our self-esteem? That is easy when you look at it right. By cultivating those who, like yourself, would rather a faithful and principled friend than a rich or popular character that cannot be relied on, you will find that the views of those outside your personal circle really don't matter.

Probably the best example that we can cite this kind of friend would be that person in your life who always speaks their mind and any criticisms that they provide are genuine areas where you could improve.

Everyone has met or kept a friend like this.

Typically, they are comfortable in themselves, and when they criticize, it is important because it comes from a genuine desire that we should prosper.

Compare this to the social butterflies who place so much value on how you dress. Those who base their self-estimation on sexual conquests or workplace promotions (often at any cost for the last two!).

These people can be amusing, but they are hardly role-models. Worse, they can drag you down to their level.

Simply put, you'll find it very hard to control

yourself and the things in your power to shape if you surround yourself with those who can't even love themselves.

Learn to appreciate yourself for the right reason.

The stern exercise of control in the things within your sphere of influence focused on the achievement of your own happiness.

Chapter 18 Amor Fati - Loving Fate Whatever Comes

It is a phrase that you may have heard, but do you know what it means?

Amor Fati is Latin for "a love of Fate".

A powerful Stoic belief, the concept Of Amor Fati is easy to understand but challenging to master. To love your fate is to not only accept EVERYTHING that has happened to you but to love it... the good parts and the bad.

So, how is this accomplished? First, remember that the Stoic doesn't see a tragedy as "bad". Everyone will die; our bodies are only loaned to us. Riches come and go. As a Stoic chooses what impressions they will take of any given situation, then they are in control of their own happiness.

By choosing to embrace every step on the path that has led you here then you can know a tranquil peace. After all, can you control Nature?

This is not to say that you should run headlong into dangerous situations like a Viking, using fate as an excuse. Instead, you should consider the whole of your fate and the lessons that have come from it. A Stoic knows that it is all about perspective.

In "Discourses" [27], we are told that whoever complains about their fate is unskilled in that art which we call life. Everything has its place in and serves the Universe as a whole.

Our bodies, especially, reacting in health or in sickness, whether we be young or old, and especially in the changes that we go through as we age.

These are things which are beyond our control, and yet our will, which IS ours to control, rebels against them.

A Stoic's attention should always be directed towards that which they can control. This attitude, combined with exercises of voluntary discomfort, allow the Stoic a special kind of mental preparation that allows for Amor Fati.

Love your fate. Don't allow yourself to be angry, nor spend so much time looking behind you that you fall over your own feet. Here are a few examples to help you to get the idea if the concept still seems a little loose:

Maybe you grew up moving all the time and never spent more than a year in the same school. Instead of seeing this as a social impediment, you might choose to embrace how self-reliant you became.

If you never knew your parents, rather than lament the lost time with them, you can consider that this required you to be strong and self-made.

If you spent a year unemployed, you've been given a crash course in the things that you want versus the things that you actually need.

Every step that you have taken in life is important and should not only be accepted, but accepted with love. Nothing is more immutable than the past, nor more instructive once you have achieved this kind of acceptance.

You cannot control your fate, but you can control how you view it.

Chapter 19 Revenge Is Not Necessary

When it comes to the subject of revenge, Seneca had some pretty good advice in his "Hardship and Happiness" treatise. He says that we should consider this kind of behavior beneath us, if even simply for the fact that there is never a shortage of people who enjoy and excel at hurting those who are injurious to others in their words and actions. [34]

Simply put, one day, the person that wronged you is going to make the mistake of wronging someone else on their own level. It's worth noting that Seneca took great pleasure in hearing of the fall of Caligula, and when asked about it, he said that one can exist quite well being opposed to revenge while still "finding some satisfaction in the outcome".

We're only human, after all!

So how does one quell the fires of the desire for revenge? There are certain exercises that can help. We've put together a few of them that you can try the next time you find yourself dearly wanting to have the last laugh.

Exercises For Calming The Mind

Ridicule - A great way to prevent a knee-jerk response when someone is really "getting your goat" is to make light of it. If revenge is on your mind so much that you have a mental list, rather than ignore it (because we all know how that works, per the "try not to think of a polar bear" example that leads to, well, polar bears), try instead to spend a few minutes in the morning making light of the ones who harmed you. Dropping cartoon anvils on their heads, visualizing them in clown "dunking booths", or if the ridiculous doesn't function, you can always try the next...

Pity Them - Someone probably has to live with this person. Do you know if that person harms them often? Perhaps they had a damaging childhood. Life deals us all different cards, and the odds are that if someone is dedicated to finding their pleasure to the detriment of others that they have failed to see the lessons of such travails. They have only chosen to take the pain from life and to redistribute it. With this in mind, you should realize that they are not worth your time. In a sense, they are dying already and they don't even know it.

Meditative Conditioning - Did you know that you can make mental associations with peaceful meditation sessions you've had? The next time that you meditate, think of a word or a combination of words to create your own mantra. As you reach a state of relaxation, repeat this mantra to yourself over and over, and try repeating it at different times throughout the day or week. With a little practice, you can condition your mind to relax quickly and this can put a stop to the "revenge fires" before they even get a chance to take hold.

Revenge is a dish best never served in the first place.

Chapter 20 Have A Daily Diary

In his text, the "Principal Doctrines", Epicurus tells us that unlimited time and limited time may both offer the same amount of pleasure if we simply measure the limits of that pleasure with reason. [35]

He has a good point.

The question, however, is how one learns to evaluate the passage of time and the benefits that one has reaped from it. A good method is to keep a daily diary.

A daily diary gives you access to your thoughts for a particular day and can be a "paper trail" of your accomplishments as well.

A great tool for memory, some even place

mnemonic devices in their journals, simple sentences such as "an eggplant purple shirt that was more interesting than a nearby argument" looks obscure to anyone else who reads it. For you, however, this "mind hack" can instantly bring a vivid memory to your mind (this technique, incidentally, is fantastic for travel as well, capturing things your pictures won't!)

So, how do you get started with a daily journal, and what should you write?

Getting started is simple. Acquire for yourself a notepad or a blank book from your local bookstore. Decide how you will be collecting your thoughts. Two Good ways of doing this are as follows:

- **Method 1** - Having a journal at home where you write down your thoughts at the end of each day. This is good because you can get an idea of what things "stuck out" in your day that might require a Stoic application of logic.

- **Method 2** - Keeping a small notepad and pen with you at all times so that you can write things down as you go. At the end of the day, you can transfer the contents of the notebook into your actual journal. This provides a bit of contemplation and also helps to put things in perspective. Ask yourself, "are these things that I can change?". Sometimes writing down our thoughts is an excellent way to determine what is truly critical and what is simply dross.

Whichever method you choose, it is recommended that you keep your journal with you at all times so that you can review it 3 times a day. Why is this so important to Stoics?

Well, by breaking down these thoughts that you have on paper, you are exercising your "logic muscles" and getting yourself in the habit of being contemplative of your actions <u>as they occur</u>.

You will be able to see in your writing if you are letting yourself be driven by base things such as anger, envy, lust, greed, and more. At the end of the week, you can even review the last 7 days and recognize trends in your thinking.

This allows you to devise strategies to divert unwanted behavior. If you are having anger issues that week, then you will know some meditation can help. If you are coveting goods, a bit of voluntary discomfort might remind you what is *truly* best.

Learning the structure of your thoughts is an important step in mastering them, and your journal will be an invaluable tool for this.

Chapter 21 Other Things That Matter

Many things are important to the Stoic way of thinking. We've compiled some of the most important in this chapter so that you will have a helpful assortment of guidelines to help you on the path of the Stoic.

Many of these things are not easy, but you MUST always strive towards achieving them. Isn't your happiness worth it?

Be Genuine, Modest And Truthful

Mark Twain may have said it best [36] when he said, "If you tell the truth, you don't have to remember anything."

It's comical but true and happens to be very important to the Stoic way of thinking. You will want to be authentic in your actions and words, humble in your demeanor, and never afraid to give someone a truth that they might not necessarily want to hear.

This doesn't mean to be vulgar, of course. Rather, it means that you should garner for yourself a reputation for being someone who gives an honest answer when their opinion is asked for. If you are worried that this might be too hard on your friends, then you can always ask, "Are you looking for support or for my opinion?"

Have Patience

Patience is the key to a number of things in your life, and a Stoic must excel at it. Learn the proper time for doing things and be tolerant of the failings of others. After all, each must walk their own path the best they can and their failings are not within your control.

Patience also has the power to diminish anger, so get in the habit of deferring your responses when the first response is obviously an emotional one. A Stoic can only be angered if they allow it, and patience will help you to manage what you allow or do not allow to get through.

Remember, "Seek not for events to happen the way that you wish. Rather, you should wish for things to happen as they do for a happier life." [38]

Pause And Take A Deep Breath

Get yourself in the habit of stopping for a deep breath or counting to 10 whenever you feel an emotional response is about to force its way out of you. This is going to take some practice (every day, in fact) and is not an ability that is easily won. It is, however, achievable if you try.

One thing that can help you is your journal.

When you feel an emotional response bubbling to the surface, push it back down and write it down.

Another method is this quick meditation exercise, courtesy of Herbert Benson, a Professor of Medicine at Harvard. He recommends listening to your breathing as you breathe slowly, aware of the breathing rhythms while thinking a word of your choosing like "Stoic", "Logic", or "Good" as a means of bringing you back to your center. [39].

Remember, if it is important, will it not still be important tomorrow? Teach yourself never to make hasty decisions, and you will be much happier for it.

Otherwise

"Otherwise" means essentially "if things were different, then...". This is actually rather profound. Have you noticed how everyone else's problems seem much easier than your own? What if you had the same problem that you just gave someone sound advice on. Would you advise yourself the same way?

You should.

There is a lesson in this. The Stoic learns to look at things like a bird, from above, to see how a problem really fits into the scope of things. Learning to distance yourself from a problem in the Stoic way will make your own problems as easy to solve as the ones you have been giving good counsel on already.

You know your own advice is good, why not learn

how to give it to yourself properly?

Speak Little And Well

If you want your words to be powerful, use fewer of them. Talking about the latest antics of a celebrity, for instance, or even a popular coworker, is wasted time. Why speculate on a stranger's life when you have enough important questions about your own? Gossip also leads to snap judgments, which we love as a species.

As a Stoic, you know that another's life is beyond your control and that there is no way that you can know the reasons behind their actions. Preferably we would advise that you push towards topics of a more challenging nature. New theories on psychology or the latest technology. Especially new modes of thought.

By limiting what you choose to say, you will make

your words more important and others will notice.

In a society where words are wasted so often, you cannot help but notice the economy of the wise. Lastly, joking is fine in moderation, but don't overdo it. As Epicurus tells us, *"If he speaks only in jest, his words are foolishness as no one will believe them."* [40]

Choose Your Company Well

In "Of Human Freedom", Epictetus says to cultivate not the company of a rich old man, but rather, a philosopher. This is good advice in general.

No, you can't choose for all of your friends to be philosophers, but you can cultivate a company with comparable values to your own. [41]

The company that you keep is important because we tend to emulate those around us to an extent. While the alternative is others emulating you, the wise choice is always going to be surrounding yourself with those who share your values. Cultivate your growth in the company you keep.

There should be no weeds in your garden.

Don't Speak Too Much About Yourself

Just as you conserve your words when it comes to gossip or celebrities, avoid telling your own stories so much. Aside from being humble, this is also a good way to focus your words on important things.

The questions of life are more important than the

telling of one's own exploits, are they not?

Answering direct questions is fine or telling how you learned something, but otherwise, you should advise, rather than advertise.

Speak Without Judging

As a Stoic, you should avoid making judgments about other people. Stick to logic. From a practical standpoint, speaking in enmity of another may earn you enmity, and if, instead, it earns you praise, do you really want the praise of someone who enjoys hurtful gossip?

Never forget that the best and brightest of us can fall in a heartbeat. Tragedy can affect anyone. Who are we to say that none have a good excuse for it? [42]

Focus On Giving Value

Do what you can for your community. You are a part of it, and you set an example for others. Do volunteer work. Help others to learn a skill. Give back to your community.

Nothing insulates us from the bad will of others more than becoming a valuable member of society.

Stoicism is not about being a hermit, after all.

Throw yourself, heart and soul, into the duty of looking out for both the community and the individual. [43]

Accept The Sacrifices

As a Stoic, you will be getting into the habit of

breaking down significant problems into smaller, more manageable problems. Part of doing this effectively is a proper understanding of sacrifice.

If you think of it in its original connotation, a sacrifice was something that you gave to the gods in exchange for something that you wanted.

Your goals are the same, especially the goal of being a true Stoic. Realize that what you want has a cost and weigh it against your goal to determine which has more value to you. What you are losing or what you will gain!

Ruthlessly Protect Your Time

A Stoic doesn't waste their time. You must find the right attitude towards Time so that you can value and allocate it wisely. [44] Those cell phone games? Looking at Facebook all day?

These are trivial things, and you are going to need to tone it down.

Certainly, there is nothing wrong with taking a little time to catch up but when these things become all-day habits, then it's time to do a little trimming. You've got more important things to do.

Live Below Your Means

Rather than falling to excess, live humbly and your life will be richer for it. Don't you like your small house? How can it be small when it provides shelter and houses your growing virtues? [45]

Prioritizing your life is the key to happiness.

It's not going to be in that new fancy television or

a sports car that moves at speeds you aren't allowed to drive in the first place. So, save the money and live humbly, defining yourself by your actions and not the things which you own.

If people choose to judge you for this, then you can bet that their priorities lie in things, not people.

Keep It Simple, Do Your Job

Just as all of nature gets up and does what it is supposed to do in the morning, so should you. Don't complicate your life with procrastination when it comes to your work and your place in society.

A Stoic knows that working hard is a key part of happiness. After all, what do people say when you are depressed?

Keep yourself busy.

Be industrious by nature, and you'll find that this attitude creeps into everything that you do. Once your work is done, the remaining time is yours, so get it out of the way!

Memento Mori

Do not fear death because it is only natural. Everyone is going to die sometime. As you cannot know when this will be, you should use this realization to spur you in hoarding your time.

Live every day as if it were your last.

It could be, you know? By recognizing this and striving to fill your time with things which you can control, managed well, you can ensure that the emptiness which some feel in life will never get close to you.

Seneca once said that Socrates' death by hemlock made him great in that it demonstrated his complete lack of the fear of death. He practiced what he preached, a Stoic until the end. When you read about Seneca's death, you can see for yourself if he was able to do the same.

Memento Mori, indeed!

Chapter 22 Daily Stoic Routine

To develop yourself as a Stoic, you are going to need to change a lot of things. We are going to start with your daily routine. We've selected several daily exercises that will help to bring your way of thinking into a sharp focus as you teach yourself how to control what you can control.

Morning Routine

Every morning you'll have four tasks to perform without fail. These exercises are vital as they are going to help you to develop insight into all of the tasks that you need to do. Not just in the doing, either.

These exercises will prepare you to expect and to deal with things when they go wrong so that you are not controlled by your own emotions when this happens. You should start with the following:

- **Meditation** - As a simple meditation to help to ground yourself in a core Stoic concept, find a comfortable place to sit, close your eyes, and start to focus on your breathing. Breathe in for a count of 6, hold it for a count of 6, and exhale for a count of 6. With each count, you should tell yourself, "I will only concern myself with the things which are within my control.". Meditate in this fashion for 10 to 15 minutes each morning and note it in your journal to keep track.

- **A View From Above** - Arrange your current life's problems in front of you and take a mental step back. Think about how these problems fit into the scope of things. Maybe you don't currently have a job, or the rent is late. Yes, these things can be stressful, but only if you let them. Realize that the world goes on and that you are exactly where you need to be.

By seeing things in their proper place, these problems will lose their stressful aspects and become what they should be. Something that you can address without stress.

- **Negative Visualization** - Take a few minutes to visualize the worst things that could happen currently. You could be penniless and homeless, for instance. Worse, a car accident could take away your ability to walk. Get creative. This Stoic exercise is designed not to be morbid, but rather to reinforce an appreciation for what you have as well as to prepare you for the worst. If the worst does come, you will have years of practice for it and you will not only endure. You will thrive.

- **Contemplation Of The Sage** - Take something that inspires you, be it a feat that impresses you or a particular person that you admire. This should be a reflection of the type of person you wish to be. Focus on this and let it inspire you throughout the day.

Daily Routine

Next, we are going to focus on things that you can do during the day to cultivate the Stoic way of thinking. Reflect this way of thinking in your actions and you will be well on your way to where you need to be.

Think of it as "flexing your Stoic muscles".

As such, a simple way to remember your daily routine until it has become a habit is to use the acronym "BICEP" (like the muscle). It is short for the following daily activities:

- *Be Aware* - Be aware of yourself and your character throughout the day. Make decisions the same way that your role model would, for instance. Be on your best behavior. A Stoic has good character, and this is something that you must develop. The first reward of a benefit is awareness of it. [45]

- *Indifference And Acceptance* - Things happen. You must accept and remind yourself that they are neither good nor bad until you have decided how you will perceive them. A job lost can be an inspiration to get something better. A relationship that didn't work out means you will be single when the right person comes around. It is all about interpretation, and the harm that comes from these things comes only when a Stoic allows them this power.

- *Cognitive Distancing* - When you feel an emotional response coming, take a deep breath, and defer it. Do not make a decision based on this emotion and if it seems overpowering, take a deep breath and remove yourself from the situation to regain your composure. It helps if you write down the emotion-based decision that you were going to make and then wait until later to read it and see if it is still what you want. Often you will find that the emotion-based decision was poorly chosen.

- *Empathetic Understanding* - When another person seems to be acting irrationally, withhold judgment, and instead tell yourself, "This is the only way that they know how to deal with this." As you cannot know their intentions, it is possible that their behavior is to be expected or not as strange as it appears. Remember that like you, another person can only do what they think is best and it is illogical to judge them for it.

- *Physical Self-Control Training* - At least once a day, tell yourself "no" or "yes". The "no" will be for a temptation, such as that extra dessert or the desire to sleep in. The "yes" should be for something outside your normal scope, like going to see that museum exhibit or a social event that you have been invited to, like a concert. It seems small, but little exercises in control may be built up to great effect over time.

Evening Routine

In the evening, a Stoic should be contemplative of the day's actions. This is a great time to write them down in your journal for future review as well, as documenting your thoughts is an excellent way to see when changes are starting to occur in them.

In the present day, the "here and now", you will want to review your actions to see where you are succeeding and where you are failing to exercise control. This is going to show you what you need to work on so that you can work on these problems with the brutal self-awareness of the Stoic.

Do these two things every evening to accomplish this:

1. **Triple Reflections** - Go over the events of your day 3 times asking yourself:

   - **Was I a "good person" today?** - Think of your role models and compare your behavior to this. Not just in the sense of "was I bad" but by thinking on your actions and how they reflected on your character during the day. This will teach you always to strive to be your best.

   - **What virtues have I followed today?** - Were you humble? Did you speak less as you have been taught? Did you defer emotional response whenever possible? At first, you may find it difficult, but by asking yourself this hard question, you will begin modifying your behavior so that you ARE exercising Stoic virtues, and you will have many to list for yourself when you contemplate this. Remember, it is easy to note or challenge another's virtues while ignoring or neglecting your own. [46]

- **Did I make thoughtful decisions today?** - Think of all of the decisions which you had to make during the day. Were these good decisions, or were they the product of emotions, temptations, or other undesirable influences? Be brutally honest with yourself. If you recognize a poor decision, then you can avoid making the same mistake twice, but if you don't force yourself to look at your actions, then you will not grow as a Stoic.

- **Did I behave irrationally today?** - Upon reviewing the events of the day thrice, is there anything that sticks out as irrational, now that it is something in the past? Irrational behavior is much easier to realize once you are "out of the moment", and by acknowledging it in the evening, you will empower yourself to defer these irrational choices when they come next time.

- **How can I improve?** - What did you not like about your day that you feel you can improve upon. Keep in mind that it needs to be something within your control. Wanting to influence anything that is not in your control is dangerous. It makes us feel powerless and we make poor decisions. Remember to base your happiness on what you can affect. So, with these things, how can you improve?

2. **Amor Fati** - Relax and take a moment to embrace your past. Realize that everything which has happened up to this point has brought you to your present.

Love this fact.

Everything that you are hinges on it, in fact. If it helps, google some of the famous people of history which you have admired and look for bad things that have happened in their lives. You should realize that everyone, great and small, can be brought low.

By accepting that this is Fate and out of our control, we can learn to love it. For what are we but the sum of our parts?

Seneca sums it up nicely, asking, *"Why should I grieve or be outraged if I meet the fate shared by all who are just a little ahead of me?"*. Love your Fate and own it, it's the Stoic way.

More Stoic Exercises To Do Throughout The Week

Aside from your daily routine, we've put together a few exercises that you can do throughout your week. Stoicism is a difficult path, but practice makes perfect, so hoard your time like a good Stoic and spend it on making yourself stronger.

Exercise 1: "Kissing A Mortal"

This one seems a bit grim if you aren't looking at it the Stoic way. Epictetus tells us when kissing a loved one, like your wife or child, that you should remind yourself that you are "kissing a mortal" because nothing is permanent, especially those we love.

You could look at this practice as a morbid thing to think, or you could try perceiving it this way: How much more will you treasure those close to you when you are daily reminding yourself of their mortality?

Nothing lasts. Possessions and people do not last. A Stoic realizes this, and as even our bodies are on loan, death was sometimes referred to as "this person was returned".

Once you recognize this, then you will be more prepared inwardly for the time when you might lose them but better than this, you will know when that happens that you appreciated them every day of your life. So, kiss your loved ones, daily, as many times as you can, and remind yourself that you are "kissing a mortal".

Exercise 2: Practicing Patience

Practicing patience doesn't have to be difficult, and you can tune-out a little in the process. The next time that you have an appointment somewhere to meet a friend, to see a movie, or anything else that is scheduled for a particular time, you should plan to arrive one or two hours early.

You can bring your cell phone but turn it to silent and resist the urge to play with it.

Bring something to read to steep yourself a little more in Stoicism. Something good from Seneca, Epictetus, or Marcus Aurelius will do the trick.

Then, simply wait for your appointment. Be at peace. Learn not to feel rushed. If you like, bring a highlighter and you can note portions of the book that you wish to contemplate later.

By making yourself wait for things, you will increase your patience at the same moments that you are learning good ways to allocate your time.

Try it!

You'll be amazed by how you feel when you aren't always in a hurry to get to something.

Exercise 3: Exercise Regimen

Building endurance boosts your body's natural strength at the same time that it enhances your patience.

It also boosts your will, because if it were easy, EVERYONE would do it.

We recommend hiring a personal trainer for once a week sessions at your local gym. Later, when you get to this, consider twice a week. If the cost of the trainer is prohibitive, go for one "trained" session and one "unsupervised" session a week, or you can do a little online research and create an exercise regimen for yourself.

Once you know what machines and various kinds of weights are available in the gym, you can even join an online exercise forum and you'll find many people willing to help you for free.

If you can do this twice a week for sessions of 30 minutes each, you will find your will sharpening up slowly and noticeably. Count on it.

Exercise 4: No-Power Weekend

Spend a weekend as if your electricity has been knocked out by a storm or you were not able to pay the bill. Get some candles in advance for light and be ready to eat things out of cans with your can opener or other items that don't need refrigeration (take your drinks out of the fridge and drink them warm, no cheating!).

This will give you an experience that people in less developed parts of the world go through all the time. Electric "brownouts" are frequent in many places, and where you live, people are experiencing the same from simple non-payment of the bill.

You should understand what that is like.

This exercise builds an appreciation for the things that you have and also will surprise you a little when you figure out that you can still keep yourself entertained. Try this exercise once or twice a month and journal your results. By candlelight, of course!

Exercise 5: Speaking Only When Spoken To

Spend a week where you only speak in response, rather than initiating or "jumping in" to other people's conversations. This is harder than it sounds, but there are a lot of rewards to this.

A Stoic learns to wield their words economically, meaning that you want to use them only when there is something important to say.

While you are doing this exercise, you will want to have a notebook handy. Make notes as you notice throughout the day what people are talking about. Make a little shorthand for your notetaking (using nicknames or numbers, for instance, will help avoid any accidental awkwardness if someone notices you writing). At the end of each day of the one-week experiment, you should evaluate what you have learned.

How many productive conversations did you hear as opposed to a celebrity or local gossip?

Do you notice how most conversations are competitions between the speakers to speak most about themselves?

Seeing how prevalent this is in your own circles is the first step to curing yourself of the same habits.

Try it and see!

Exercise 6: Volunteer Work

Commit one day a week to volunteer work for a month. It can be anything you like. You can help at your local library, for instance. You can help out at a homeless shelter. Find a group that is doing carpentry work for folks with lesser income.

What you do is up to you, but do it.

As a Stoic, you must learn to be a strong

contributor to your community. Also, don't brag about it. Remember to be humble. You can tell someone if they ask, for instance, "Why can't you go out on Saturday?" but unless directly asked, don't advertise.

Help your community not to look good but to BE good.

For the Stoic, the act is the reward.

Exercise 7: Embrace Minimalism

Get yourself a notepad, and over the weekend, do an inventory of things that you have at home that you simply don't need. We're not talking about sentimental items, rather things that you could live just fine without.

Break down your clothes wardrobe, for instance,

and donate the excess to the Salvation Army. Do you really need 10 or more pairs of shoes? There's another suitable target for you. Items you are storing in another room in the house on the off-chance that you'll need them again, these should go too.

A Stoic counts their blessings and understands that there is very little that we actually need. Try this exercise to get rid of a bit of excess that you are hanging on to, and if you like the feeling (which you will if you do it, trust us on this), we would highly recommend reading up on minimalism.

There are many tips and tricks both in books and online that can help you to get all that excess out and focus simply on what you need.

Live humbly and appreciate what you have, you're only "borrowing it", after all. You can only own your own happiness.

Exercise 8: Emotional Journal

You can do this with a separate journal (or simply use a different color ink so that these entries stick out). For a month, write down anything that provokes the urge for an emotional response.

Do this whether you were able to resist it or not (also note how you reacted) and write down what anything that happened earlier that day, which you think contributed to your emotional response.

At the end of the month, spend some time reviewing this. Do you notice any trends in the types of things that "set you off"? If the emotional response is the result of a building-up of events earlier in the day, then you can work on deferring your responses to these events so that you can learn to take different impressions from them.

For instance, if someone is mean in the morning, you can take offense or allow yourself to be hurt, or think to yourself that this person is obviously having a bad day and is limited to expressing themselves in this way. If you can't get coffee in the morning, you could be unhappy and complain about it or take it as a cue that maybe juice is a good start for this day.

Keeping an emotional journal and attempting to note "triggers" will slowly give you a proper picture of why you behave the way that you do.

Once you know your triggers, then YOU can begin preparing for them so that you are in control of how you choose to perceive them.

Exercise 9: Virtue Of The Day

Dedicate the day for looking for a chance to exercise a particular virtue. Cultivation of virtues comes from practice. Some example virtues you might work on:

- **Courage** - Do something that daunts you. Go on a social outing that you would typically avoid from fear. Speak more in a work meeting when you are normally silent. Basically, go out of your comfort zone for a moment to exercise your courage.

- **Temperance** - Spend the day enjoying the little things. There is an abundance in having your needs met that we tend to forget in this age of excess. Have an apple outside on a bench in the park, for instance. Pack a nice lunch and skip that restaurant on your lunch break. Live on less to live more.

- **Justice** - Pay extra special attention to how you treat and interact with others. Make an extra effort to be "fair" in all of your dealings. Focusing on this virtue can be quite enlightening, as sometimes we are unfair to others without realizing it. Pay a little extra attention, and see what you learn from it.

- **Wisdom** - Take a little time reading Epictetus or some of the other core texts and then try to find some recommendations that you can "try on the field". For example, where we are told to be careful of the company we keep, you could exercise this principle by trying to spend more time that day around people who are good for you. In this, we would recommend getting a copy of "Discourses" as listed in our Bibliography. You will find many practical instructions which you can easily apply in everyday life. Examples such as getting in the habit of not making promises, ignoring rumors, and more!

Exercise 10: Analysis Of The Past

One way to help to inspire yourself to wait before making decisions is this. Make yourself a small notepad where you make a list of poor decisions that you have made, which were much clearer later. Don't make this into an excuse to be sad.

Simple things like "I shouldn't have started that business without researching" or "I shouldn't have gotten a pet that I didn't have time for" are good examples. Decisions that are emotional produce an arguably large portion of stress in our lives.

By carrying around a quick-reference in your pocket, you have a physical reminder that you can call on when you "feel an emotional decision coming on".

It is good to give yourself a reminder that mistakes can be easily made and that most often, these lapses in judgment are due to emotion.

Once a week, write down five bad decisions in the notebook (it should be pocket-sized) and add to it for a month. At the end of this month, start adding current "bad decisions" as you make them. What do the older entries and the current ones tell you?

While it seems a bit basic, this is actually a perfect way to be more mindful of your decisions and to highlight any particular triggers that you will want to address. Write it, be honest, and learn from it!

Chapter 23 Watch Day-To-Day Improvements

Gauging your progress is a slow process, but it is something that you will want to do.

Think of it like erosion. A process of nature that means trickles of rainwater can one day sculpt mighty canyons.

Your daily routines will help to enforce the application of logic and a slow but growing mastery over knee-jerk emotional responses.

This is not only achievable; it is inevitable if you set yourself on the Stoic path and stick with it. Some things that you may notice as you go:

- **Interactions With Others Will Become More Productive** - By learning to defer emotion-based decisions and reactions, you will find that you can get more done. People tend to prod others into making emotional responses, often to take control of a situation. By taking a deep breath first or even deferring an important response by a day so that you can analyze the facts, YOU will be the one in control, and others will notice that you tend to get things done.

- **You Will Take More Notice Of Others Making Emotion-Based Decisions** - As you get into the habit of making decisions based on sense instead of "sensation", there is a curious side effect. When someone around you makes a poor decision that is obviously emotionally motivated, it will stick out like a sore thumb. Resist the urge to advise them at this point unless you are asked. You still have a lot of learning to do and a Stoic should remain humble.

- **Prioritization Of Your Goals Provides A Feeling Of Security** - In general, that sense of "I don't know where I'm going" is not so much a lack of concrete goals as it is the presence of too many ill-defined goals to succeed realistically. Through prioritizing your goals and sacrificing the things you don't need, you will always know in which direction you are headed. It is a good feeling.

- **You'll Shine Brighter Once You Don't Need To** - Once the only person you are trying to impress is yourself, then you will start to stick out from the pack. This is because of the rarity of people who define themselves with actions rather than words. Help your community, orient on your goals, speak less. People cannot help but notice a quiet depth of character.

- **Involvement In Your Community Will Lead To A Better Quality Of Friends** - By giving back to your community you will come in touch with others who have a deep care for giving back and helping to build a better community. Associate with these people as much as possible. A Stoic is a model "citizen".

- **Others Will Start Asking You For Advice** - As your self-discipline and careful decision-making skills become apparent, people are going to notice it. They will know that you are focused, you are dependable. You are in charge of your happiness and not wasteful of time. They are going to start asking you questions, so get used to it. Advise them and tell them how you've come to your conclusions. It is good practice to examine your own logic out loud and it is instructive to others as well!

Conclusion

In this book, we have explored what Stoicism means as well as how you can use it to strengthen your willpower, resist the impulse to make emotional decisions, and own your own happiness. We would advise you to do the exercises that we have taught you as often as possible because Stoicism is not something that you can pick up in a weekend. Philosophy is a way of life and like everything, there will be sacrifices involved in achieving your happiness. So, start doing your exercises TODAY. Keep track of your progress with your journal and in time, you will begin to see the rewards that your hard labors have earned. So will everyone else, in fact, but this is going to take time.

For now, remember not to advertise your Stoicism. People like to critique everything that you do, and you won't do yourself any favors by giving them a chance to erode a foundation that you are still building. Stay silent and learn. Let the Stoic in you be shown in your actions. Stay humble and tenacious and before you know it, you'll be advising others about the way of the Stoic!

References

[1] Epictetus; Translation by Robert Dobbin; "Discourses and selected writings" pp.468.5,

- [3] pp.499.7
- [4] pp.498.2
- [5] pp.461.7
- [6] pp.474.5
- [7] pp.491.6
- [9] pp.393.8
- [10] pp.498.9
- [12] pp.479.7
- [13] pp.336.2
- [14] pp.497.5
- [15] pp.492.3
- [16] pp.472.2
- [18] pp.461.1
- [19] pp.497.6
- [20] pp.155.4
- [21] pp.502.7
- [23] pp.485.1
- [26] pp.480.6

- [27] pp.480.6
- [28] pp.449.9
- [30] pp.208
- [32] pp.499.5
- [33] pp.338.7

[2] Marcus Aurelius; Produced by Robert Nield, Tom Allen, Charles Franks and the Online Distributed Proofreading Team "The Meditations of the Emperor Marcus Aurelius Antonius" pp132.7

- [17] pp.209.2

[8] Seneca; "Moral Letters to Lucilius - Letter 18" "XVIII. On Festivals and Fasting"; "Epistulae Morales ad Lucilium/Letters from a Stoic"

[11] Seneca; Translated by Robert A. Caster and Martha C. Russbaum; "Anger, Mercy, and Revenge"; pp.67

[22] Marcus Aurelius; Translated by George Long "Book 5";"The Meditations of the Emperor Marcus Aurelius Antonius" pp.20

- [24] " pp.9
- [25] pp.13
- [31] pp.21

[29] Penguin classics; "Seneca - Letters from a Stoic" pp 23.5

[34] Translated by Elaine Fantham, Harry M. Hine, James Ker, and Gareth D, Williams; Seneca; "Hardship and Happiness", pp. 198

[35] Translated by Robert Drew Hicks; Epicurus - Principle Doctrines; pp.1

[36] Loving, Jerome - "MARK TWAIN: THE ADVENTURES OF SAMUEL L. CLEMENS"

[37] Seddon, Keith - Chapter 33, 'Epictetus' Handbook and the Tablet of Cebes

[38] Edited by Patrick Ussher; "Stoicism Today Selected Writings, Volume 1", pp.210.4

[39] Robert, Donald, "Stoicism and the Art of Happiness" pp.142.9

[40] Translated by Robert Drew Hicks, Epicurus, "LETTER TO MENOECEUS", pp. 24

[41] Translated by Robert Dobbin, Epictetus, 'Of Human Freedom' pp.130

[42] Edited by John M. Cooper and J.F. Procope; Seneca, "Moral and Political essays', pp.101

[43] Penguin Classics, Seneca, "Dialogues and Letters", pp.120.4

[44] Translated by Harry M. Hine; Seneca, "Natural Questions"; pp.8

[45] Translated by Miriam Griffin and Brad Inwood; Seneca, "On Benefits", pp. 83

[46] Translation by Elaine Fantham, Seneca, "Selected Letters", pp.10

[47] Translation by Brad Inwood, "Selected Philosophical Letters"; pp.28

Reference Sourcebooks

1. Epictetus; Discourses
2. Marcus Aurelius ' Meditations of the Emperor

3. Letters to a Stoic

4. Anger, mercy, and revenge

5. Seneca - Hardship and Happiness

6. Epicurus - Principle Doctrines; pp.1

7. Loving, Jerome - "MARK TWAIN: THE ADVENTURES OF SAMUEL L. CLEMENS"

8. Seddon, Keith - Chapter 33, 'Epictetus' Handbook and the Tablet of Cebes

9. Epictetus, 'Of Human Freedom'

10. Edited by Patrick Ussher; "Stoicism Today Selected Writings, Volume 1",

11. Robert, Donald, "Stoicism and the Art of Happiness"

12. Translated by Robert Drew Hicks, Epicurus, "LETTER TO MENOECEUS", pp. 24

13. Edited by John M. Cooper and J.F. Procope; Seneca, "Moral and Political essays'

14. Penguin Classics, Seneca, "Dialogues and Letters"

15. Translation by John Davie, Seneca, "Dialogues and Essays"

16. Penguin Classics, Seneca, "On the shortness of life

17. Translated by Harry M. Hine; Seneca, "Natural Questions"

18. Seneca, "On Benefits"

19. Translation by Elaine Fantham, Seneca, "Selected Letters"

20. Translation by Brad Inwood, "Selected Philosophical Letters"

Disclaimer

The information contained in this book and its components, is meant to serve as a comprehensive collection of strategies that the author of this book has done research about. Summaries, strategies, tips and tricks are only recommendations by the author, and reading this book will not guarantee that one's results will exactly mirror the author's results.

The author of this book has made all reasonable efforts to provide current and accurate information for the readers of this book. The author and its associates will not be held liable for any unintentional errors or omissions that may be found.

The material in the book may include information by third-parties. Third-party materials comprise of opinions expressed by their owners. As such, the author of this book does not assume responsibility or liability for any third-party material or opinions.

The publication of third-party material does not constitute the author's guarantee of any information, products, services, or opinions contained within third-party material. Use of third-party material does not guarantee that your results will mirror our results. Publication of such third-party material is simply a recommendation and expression of the author's own opinion of that material.

Whether because of the progression of the Internet, or the unforeseen changes in company policy and editorial submission guidelines, what is stated as fact at the time of this writing may become outdated or inapplicable later.